IMAGES OF ENGLAND

KINGSWOOD
AND TWO MILE HILL

REGENT ST KINGSWOOD. 632.

IMAGES OF ENGLAND

KINGSWOOD
AND TWO MILE HILL

JILL WILLMOTT

TEMPUS

Frontispiece: Regent Street, Kingswood, *c.* 1910. To the left is the entrance to the Moravian Church. The lamp post to the right marks what is now London Street.

First published 2004

Tempus Publishing Limited
The Mill, Brimscombe Port,
Stroud, Gloucestershire, GL5 2QG
www.tempus-publishing.com

© Jill Willmott, 2004

The right of Jill Willmott to be identified as the Author
of this work has been asserted in accordance with the
Copyrights, Designs and Patents Act 1988.

British Library Cataloguing in Publication Data.
A catalogue record for this book is available from the British Library.

ISBN 0 7524 3311 3

Typesetting and origination by Tempus Publishing Limited.
Printed in Great Britain.

Contents

Acknowledgements

I gratefully acknowledge the help of all the following in preparing this book:
Mr W.D. Payne, Mrs S.C. Payne, Mrs B. Bush, Derek and Janet Fisher, Mr R. Reeves, Mr J. Bartlett, Mr J. Merrett, Mrs F. Gearing, Mrs P. Dorgan, Mr Bill Douglas, Harvey Myers IV, Mr Wally Ball, Mr R.B. Leonard, Mr F. Small, David Gapper, Mrs D. Gunningham, Mrs B. Gardiner, Mr T. Zahringer, Nigel Bull, Dennis Hill, Latham Autos Tom Garland, Paul Bridgeman, Mrs G. Parker and the ladies from The Orchard Medical Centre, Kingswood Library, Kingswood Museum and Bristol Central Library.

Special thanks go to Mike Tozer for his endless patience. Ian 'Moggsy' Gardiner and Paul Willmott for their endless trips to the library and David Stephenson for his endless nagging; without his encouragement this book would never have been written.

My very special thanks also go to Colin Hawkins. My morning spent with him in the forge was, without doubt, the highlight of writing this book. Being able to see first hand the traditional ways of the blacksmith and the wonderful smell of the forge 'in action' is an experience I will treasure for ever.

The very nature of this book means that not everything can be included in one volume. Kingswood is an historic area, there is much more to discover and I hope to write further books on Kingswood and the surrounding area. If you have any photographs, memories or newspaper cuttings of Kingswood, please do not hesitate to contact me – I will be interested to see them.

Jill Willmott
9 Quarry Road
Kingswood
Bristol
BS15 8PA

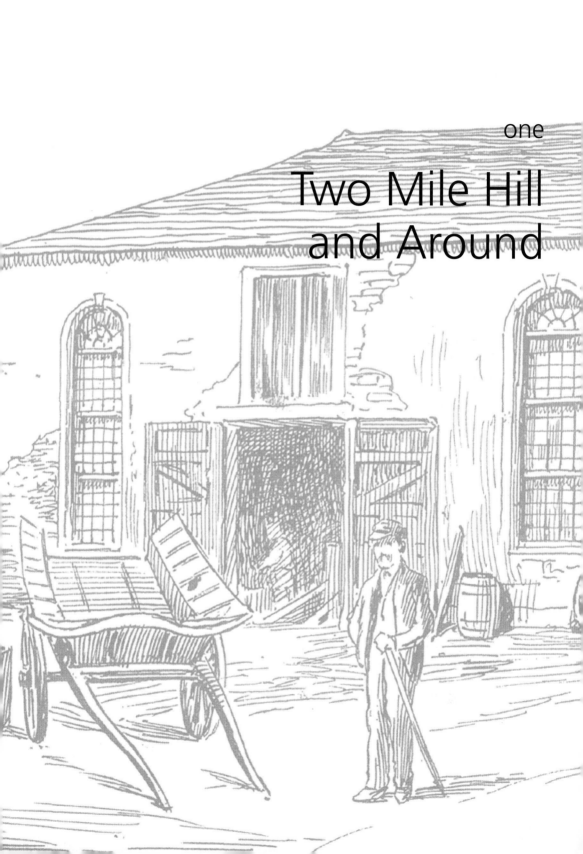

one

Two Mile Hill
and Around

A Temperance procession as it passes Rose Cottage, *c.* 1905. Rose Cottage, which stood on Two Mile Hill at its junction with Rodney Road, is behind the large hedge on the right.

Rose Cottage was the birthplace, in 1831, of John William Stone Dix. Mr Dix was largely responsible for the removal of the old Swing Bridge over the River Frome at St Augustine's and the design of Colston Avenue and the gardens at the Tramway Centre. The house was demolished in the 1970s but the large tree shown in the photograph is still standing. Behind the house were outbuildings where Invicta car batteries were made. This business was owned by Mr Walton and Mr Sweeting. The field beyond was also once part of the property, a portion of which was bought by Bethel Chapel for use as a sports field.

Right: The New Inn, Nos 9 and 11 Queen Street, Two Mile Hill, *c.* 1927. This was owned by Mr Herbert Bryant, beer retailer. By 1938 Mrs Alice Bryant was the owner and the premises had become a grocers shop.

Below: The Kingsway Cinema on Two Mile Hill was opened in 1928 at a cost of £9,000. It had a balcony, which is still in place, and could seat 800 people. There were two entrances, the left-hand door for downstairs – the 'one and nines' – and the right-hand door for the balcony. There was a '2d rush' on Saturday mornings when westerns and cartoons would be shown. The cinema closed in 1959 and became a car showroom but before it could open, tons of concrete had to be pumped in to level the sloping floor of the auditorium.

The Rose and Crown at the junction of Burchells Green Road and Two Mile Hill. Although the present building displays the date of 1905, there has been an inn on this site for well over 200 years. Records show that inquests into mining fatalities in the area were heard there as early as 1795.

Two Mile Hill at its junction with Burchells Green Road (left) and Kingsway Avenue (right), c. 1926. The Rose and Crown, then tied to Ashton Gate Brewery, stands to the left. To the right is The Prince Albert, an old pub with a reputation for backroom boxing.

Right: William Sampson, fruiterer, greengrocer and general stores, stood at 139 Two Mile Hill. The Sampson family owned market gardens on Footshill and much of the produce they sold was home grown. This picture is from around 1940.

Below: Lansdown House, *c.* 1930. This off-licence stood at No. 145 Two Mile Hill at its junction with King Street. As well as selling beer, it also sold a range of home-cooked meats.

Evangel Mission is tucked away in King Street, just off Two Mile Hill. The Mission began in 1881 when a group of Christian men decided that they could better serve both God and the community by forming a band. In the beginning they spent much of their time practising with the local Salvation Army bandsmen, although they did play at other churches and charitable functions. In 1884 a brass band contest was held at Frenchay in connection with a Temperance Fête. An unusual rule was made by the committee that bands entering the contest were to play in the procession without fee but bands not competing would receive payment. On the day of the fête several bands took part in the procession but only Evangel Band mounted the stand for the competition, the others deciding that it was better to take the money than risk the judges' decision!

The Salvation Army had rules and regulations for bandsmen and in 1888 the men were asked to sign them or cease to play at Salvation Army services. They decided that they preferred to remain free and so began the Kingswood Evangel Brass Band. There were nine original members and they conducted open-air services throughout the district. Although originally there had been no intention to build a Mission Hall, after about twelve months or so it was felt that a non-denominational mission would benefit the district and land was bought in King Street. A timber-framed, galvanised building was erected that became known locally as the 'Tin Mission'.

The first services were held in the hall in December 1889 and continued there for about ten years until a more permanent building was constructed. The 'Tin Mission' was dismantled and re-erected at Granny's Lane, Mount Hill.

In 1908, the band entered the Malborough Band Competition. They had practised for weeks, but just a couple of days before the competition, one of the bandsmen fell from a pear tree and broke his arm. Nevertheless, he was so keen to play that he travelled to Malborough with his arm in a sling and had to be lifted onto the bandstand. The band won two first prizes. On their arrival back at Two Mile Hill at almost midnight, crowds of people gathered in the streets to cheer as the band played their way back to the Mission Hall.

Group photograph outside Evangel Mission, *c.* 1900. With the outbreak of the First World War, fourteen of Evangels men were called up. However, by combining with Kingswood Town Band they were able to play to support the Red Cross and wartime fundraising events. The band was seen regularly in the district and were especially popular at the Whitsuntide processions.

In 1982 the Mission fell victim to an arsonist. All that was left after the fire were the outside walls. Services were held temporarily in the Parish Hall of St Michael's Church. The Mission reopened in May 1984 at a cost of almost £34,000. Evangel Mission is thought to be the only Mission hall in the country to have been built and supported by a band.

The Kingswood Evangel Prize Band, 1920s.

A float decorated by Evangel Mission and showing the Severn Bridge, passing the Kingswood Hotel on the corner of Hanham Road in 1966. It is followed by a float from Ebenezer Independent Methodist Church in Bell Hill Road, now demolished.

In Loving Memory of
Rev R. J. BATEMAN,
OF FLORIDA, U.S.A.
FORMERLY OF STAPLE HILL, BRISTOL,
WHO CONDUCTED REVIVAL SERVICES
IN THIS HALL MARCH 1912,
SAILED ON THE ILL-FATED TITANIC,
APRIL 10TH 1912.

TELL ME THE OLD, OLD STORY
OF UNSEEN THINGS ABOVE,
OF JESUS AND HIS GLORY,
OF JESUS AND HIS LOVE.

Robert Bateman was born in 1860, the son of a cabinet maker from Oldbury Court. Robert had travelled to America and become a Baptist minister by the time he was twenty-one years old. In 1912 he had returned to Bristol to place a headstone on his mother's grave. Whilst here, in March of that year, he conducted revival services at Evangel Mission. He was, by all accounts, a fiery preacher, but known simply as 'Uncle Bob' to the children of the districts of East Bristol.

There is no known record of what Robert Bateman preached at the meetings but he must have made a considerable impact on his congregation as, when he left to return to America with his sister-in-law, Mrs Ada Ball, many of them turned out to march before him to Staple Hill station to begin his journey home. The procession, of course, included the band and as he entered the station Mr Ebenezer Cozens, later to become Lord Mayor of Bristol, gave a solo performance on his euphonium of 'Rocked in the Cradle of the Deep'.

The choice for the solo was strangely prophetic for on 12 April 1912, Rev. Bateman sailed from Southampton on the ill-fated White Star liner *Titanic*. Rev Bateman travelled second class, his ticket, number 1166, cost £12 10s 6d. Captain Edward Smith, knowing of his passenger's reputation, asked him to conduct a Sunday service with the ships band. It was on 14 April that the ship struck an iceberg in some of the calmest seas her officers had seen. Revd Bateman supervised his sister-in-law into the lifeboat saying, 'If I don't meet you again in this world, I will in the next'. As the boat was lowered, he took off his necktie and threw it to her as a keepsake. Ada later recalled: 'Brother forced me into the last boat and threw his overcoat over my shoulders as the boat was being lowered away and as we neared the water, he took off his black neck tie and threw it to me with the words, "Goodbye. God Bless You."

It is said that Robert Bateman conducted the band as the ship sank. They struck up 'Nearer my God to Thee' and passengers and crew unable to get to the lifeboats joined in. As the liner was about to go under the hymn changed to 'Abide With Me' with Revd Bateman still conducting as the ship went down.

His body was recovered by the cable-laying vessel *Mackay-Bennett* and he was interred in the Evergreen Cemetery in Jacksonville, Florida on 12 May 1912. His memorial tablet hangs in Evangel Mission Hall.

Opposite, above: Evangel Mission leads the Whitsuntide procession through Kingswood. This picture was taken on 30 May 1966 as the procession reached Holy Trinity Church. Each church or chapel had its own banners, decorated in rich reds, blues and gold, with silk tassels and often showing a picture of the church or its founder. The banners were extremely heavy and were usually carried by two men wearing leather shoulder straps with cups to support the weight.

The funeral procession for Alfred Potter, in Burchells Green Road, 1915.

Right: The grave of Pte Potter stands on the south side of St Michaels church. In November 2003, David Stephenson and I visited his grave just before Remembrance Day and placed our own small tribute to someone we both feel we have come to know.

Above, far right: Alfred George Potter was born in 1893 in Burchills Green Road, Two Mile Hill. The cottage still stands today near the Lamb & Lark public house. Alfred's parents were Stanley Whitfield and Sarah Ann Potter. His father was an outworker in the boot trade, making boots at home. Alfred started work at the British American Tobacco Company in Bristol. He was engaged to be married when he enlisted in the 1st/4th Battalion Gloucestershire Regiment in 1914. He was sent to Danbury Training Camp in Essex and then on to France. Sadly he was injured and returned home to England where he died from his wounds. His funeral was a show of respect and compassion for a local boy who was loved by the community in which he lived. Hundreds of people lined the route for the funeral procession and there are at least eight known postcards of the event. His story has interested me and those I have told of it for many years. At last I feel I have come to know a little of who he was and why these postcards were produced. They were a memento, a mark of respect for a brave and much-loved local hero.

Opposite, below: From the *Western Daily Press*, 24 May 1915: Military Funeral at Two Mile Hill. The funeral of Pte Alfred George Potter, a young soldier of the 4th Gloucesters who was well known and esteemed in the Two Mile Hill district brought a crowded attendance to Two Mile Hill Church on Saturday (22 May 1915).

Detachments from Bristol's Own and the 1st/4th Gloucesters accompanied the gun carriage and four horses on which was the coffin covered with the Union Jack.

Colonel Rutler was unable to be present and he was represented by Acting Adjutant Whitwill accompanied by Lt Plum.

The deceased was wounded in France and expired soon after reaching Brighton Hospital.

Around the church entrance was the St Michaels contingent of Boy Scouts. The Vicar, the Rev. A.F. Adams officiated and the surpliced choir sang the hymns *Abide With Me* and *When Our Heads are Bowed with You*.

En route to the churchyard the band of Bristol's Own and The Drum and Fife Band of the 4th Gloucesters played funeral music and during the church service the organist played 'The Dead March' in 'Saul' and Chopin's 'Funeral March'. The hymn sung at the graveside was 'O God Our Help'.

The principal mourners were Mr Stanley Potter (Father) Messrs Thomas, George, Tom, John, Sam and Joe Bright (cousins) Gilbert Sumerhill and George Hale.

There were many wreaths. One was from St Michael's Bible Class of which the deceased was a member and there was another from the British American Tobacco Company with which firm he was employed prior to his joining the army and going to the Front.

An inscription on the coffin stated his age as twenty-two. Mr S. Boulton of Kingswood was the undertaker.

The church of St Michael the Archangel was consecrated by the Bishop of Bristol and Gloucester on 22 August 1848. The stone used in the building of the church was quarried from within the parish on which it stands. Close inspection of the weather vane reveals a bullet hole that has been there since the blitz on Bristol during the Second World War. The hole is horizontal to the ground proving that it was made during an aerial battle.

Above: The junction of Two Mile Hill with New Queen Street and Kingsway showing tram No. 17 entering the single track section towards St George, 4 August 1939. The sign to the left advertises A.S. Payne, plumber.

Opposite, below: Jones and Bence Motor Body Builders yard showing, in the background, what was once Robert Charleton's schoolroom, *c.* 1930s. It still stands – part of the building has been demolished and the outside has been rendered – but from the inside you can still see the arches of the windows and also the outline of the large glass door.

Robert Charleton was a Bristol Quaker who set up a pin factory adjoining Fillwood House at the Two Mile Hill end of Charlton Road, known in those days as Pin Factory Lane, to give work to the poor people of Kingswood. The factory opened in the early 1830s and, in 1841, records show that 110 women and fifty boys were employed, with 500 women and children as outworkers. Robert Charleton built a school on Two Mile Hill for his workers and their families, the only factory school in the district. On Sundays it was used as a chapel. It cost 2d a week to attend, with an extra 1d to learn to write. Robert Charleton was a generous man involved in the founding of many local chapels including Bethel in St George. He was also one of a Quaker delegation that went to Russia in 1854 to try and prevent the Tsar from entering the Crimean War. The business was eventually taken over by a Mr Lambert who lived in Fillwood House and the factory became known locally as 'Lamberts' or the 'Fillwood Factory'.

This drawing by Loxton from the early 1900s is the only known picture of Robert Charleton's schoolroom in its entirety. It shows it in use as the premises of wheelwright Mr W. Jones. The Jones family owned premises in the Two Mile Hill area from at least the 1780s.

Telephones {Kingswood 85 / Kingswood 323}

WM. JONES & BENCE

Motor Body Builders, Agents

AND

Coach Builders

ANY MAKE of MOTOR SUPPLIED

—PRIVATE OR COMMERCIAL—

REPAIRS AND RE-PAINTING

AUTHORISED FORD DEALERS

FIT (J.&B.) MOTOR BODIES

TWO MILE HILL, BRISTOL

Established over 150 years

Above left: Inside the old schoolroom, showing the arched windows, 2004.

Above right: Advertisement for Jones & Bence, *c.* 1934.

Opposite, above: Messrs Jones and Bence Motor Body Builders in the early 1930s. The first mention of Mr Bence's partnership with Mr Jones appears in Kelly's Directory for 1930. This photograph shows Robert Charleton's schoolroom, with the large arched windows, in the background to the right (now Latham Autos) and the large showroom and offices which stood where the car sales yard stands today.

Opposite, below: The same site in 2004. The building to the left, Latham Autos, is the old schoolroom building.

Fillwood AFC 1899/1900 season. The players are, back row, from left to right: G. Roberts, R. Pool, A. Reeves. G. Hales (V. Capt), F. Pratt (Asst Sec.). Middle row: P. Peters, H. Iles (Capt), G. Long, H. Caines, A. Gingell. Font row: G. Smith (Sec.), R. Stone, W. Davis.

Opposite, above: Kingswood Reformatory School, showing John Wesley's Chapel which was demolished in 1919. The school was opened under the direction of John Wesley in 1748 for the sons of miners and other poor people of Kingswood. The school moved to Lansdown in 1851 and in 1852 Mary Carpenter founded her reformatory school here. Discipline was brutal. Several older Kingswood residents can remember the screams of the boys as they were given the cat o' nine tails. There are even stories of salt being rubbed into the open wounds. It is said that the band played loudly on Sunday mornings to save local residents from hearing the screams.

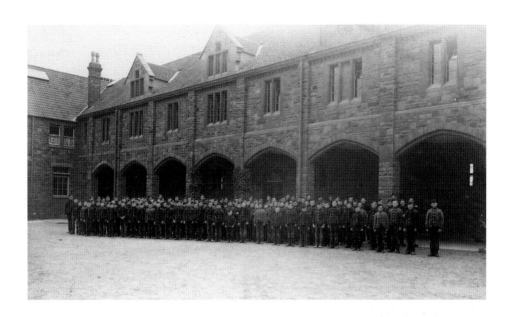

A group of boys at the Reformatory School, early 1900s. Despite being outside the parish boundary, Reformatory boys attended St Michael's church, often causing chaos. This is an extract from a letter from the Revd Baylee to Canon Ellacombe at Bitton in around 1885:

In addition to the destruction of property and disturbance caused by the boys coming and going from the church, we have the musical portions of the service destroyed by the way in which they sometimes sing entirely out of tune with the choir. There is also the horrible nuisance caused continually by their making water in the pews. The smell in the church sometimes is abominable.

It was eventually decided that the boys should attend Kingswood parish church.

The Forge, Reformatory Road off Two Mile Hill in what is now known as Kennard Road. Children on their way to Two Mile Hill School would stop to watch the blacksmith at work and were made welcome but had to stand back. Sparks would fly across the forge and when the white-hot shoes were put into the water tank to cool and the hissing sound was tremendous. The horses were actually shod in a shed at the left side of the forge in Sculls Barton. Walter Baker (far left) was a Master Farrier and Samuel Baker (far right) was the proprietor, c. 1930.

Mr and Mrs Samuel Baker outside their fruit, vegetable and shellfish shop at No. 235 Two Mile Hill. Mrs Baker cooked the cockles, mussels and crabs herself and the shells were thrown down in the back garden to make a path.

This was one of the last shops in East Bristol to sell sand for housewives. The sand was used on the stone floors in the days before wooden floorboards and carpet. It is recalled that the room behind the shop had a coal fire burning in the grate all day long. There was a mantelpiece over the grate with pegs so that wet coats (mantles) could be dried, c. 1930.

On 25 October 2003 a blue plaque to the memory of Eric Ball was unveiled at the Salvation Army Chapel by Mr Wally Ball and the Lord Mayor of Bristol, Cllr Bill Martin. Eric Ball was born on 31 October 1903 above his family's shop at Two Mile Hill. His family were all members of the Salvation Army and he played with many bands throughout the district. In 1926 he married Olive Dorset and was also appointed bandmaster at Southall and conductor of the National Orchestra. He did many arrangements for brass band and wrote many pieces of music. His works are still played all over the world. In 1937 he conducted the massed bands at the Coronation Festival and in 1969 he was awarded the OBE for services to music. He died on 1 October 1989. The Salvation Army Chapel was built in 1841 as a Primitive Methodist Chapel. The date on the building, 1879, is the date when the Salvation Army took over the premises.

Above and right: The White Horse public house at No. 264 Two Mile Hill stood between the Salvation Army Chapel and the Kings Head pub. To the right of the White Horse, next to the chapel, was a milliners shop owned by Mrs Spencer. To the left of the pub was a five-barred gate which led into a field and there were also some cottages and a sweet shop. Next to these stood the White Lion at No. 282, a small one-room pub. The left-hand door was the 'bottle and jug' and the right-hand door led to the bar. This whole rank of buildings was demolished to make way for new housing.

Opposite below, left and right: The shop of W. Hemmings, family butcher (left) at Myrtle House, No. 271 Two Mile Hill, *c.* 1912. The shop is now Eastern Spice, an Indian restaurant, seen here in 2004.

Mrs Beatrice Crewe with her dog Paddy, outside the shop at No. 276 Two Mile Hill. The shop sold sweets and tobacco and had a couple of chairs inside where you could sit and have a cup of tea. Crewe's made their own ice cream and had several pedal trolleys that sold ice cream around the district. Above the shop was the Kingsway Billiard Club, mid-1930s.

Bryants Ironmongers at No. 295 Two Mile Hill was run by a father and two sons. The shop always smelt of paraffin. This photograph was taken in the 1980s.

Clarks pie shop at No. 301 Two Mile Hill. The Kingswood shop was opened in the 1950s. The secret recipe of the Clarks pie was the key to its success. The Kingswood shop closed in 2002 but there is still a branch at Redfield.

Ernie G Williams fruit and veg shop, No. 315 Two Mile Hill, at the junction of Broadfield Avenue, c. 1981. Mr G Williams delivered locally and kept a horse and cart in the small yard behind the shop. He sold the best quality fruit and vegetables, displaying everything in the box in which it was transported. The shop was owned by at least two generations of the family.

Above: Two Mile Hill at its junction with John Street, to the left, *c.* 1938.

Left: Bourne Chapel was built in 1873 and named after Hugh Bourne, one of the founders of the Primitive Methodist Movement. The building cost £2,249 and could seat 600 people. It was later to become part of the 'Fantasie Foundations' factory and is now back in use as a place of worship under the name of Bristol Community Church.

George Bryant Britton was born on 24 July 1857, the son of Samuel Britton. Bryant & Britton, founded in the mid-1870s, was the beginnings of G.B. Britton & Sons, boot manufacturers. By 1880 'G.B.' had gone into partnership with George Jefferies and had built a small factory in Waters Road containing between fifteen and twenty sewing machines and three crude sole presses, all treadle operated. In 1900, the business moved to new premises in Lodge Road. This large factory survived until 2003, when it was demolished to make way for housing.

During the First World War, production was mainly of army boots. After the war, G.B.'s son G.E. Britton shouldered much of the responsibility when his brother died and his father became ill. He was helped from 1927 by his stepbrother J.H. Britton.

G.B. Britton died of a seizure on 11 July 1929 when attending the annual meeting of the National Federation of Shoe Manufacturers.

He was a 'hands on' manager who demonstrated how the job should be done and was often found on the shop floor with his sleeves rolled up, helping out. He knew all of his employees by name and had a great sense of humour, telling stories in a broad Gloucestershire accent. All of his life, he lived just a stone's throw from his factory. He loved the game of cricket and later in life, golf. He had been a Justice of the Peace for twenty-four years and was both Lord Mayor of Bristol and MP for East Bristol during the early 1920s. He also took an active part in bringing the electric tramway to Kingswood. However, the duty that was closest to his heart was that of Sunday School Superintendent at Zion Chapel, a post that he held for some forty-two years. He is buried in the churchyard there.

Above left: G.B. Britton as Lord Mayor of Bristol, 1920–21.

Opposite, above: 'Lodgeside', home of G.B. Britton, on Lodge Road near to Cossham Hospital. For many years it was used as part of the social club of G.B. Britton Ltd and it was demolished in 2003 to make way for new housing.

Kingswood Cricket Club at Lodgeside during the 1898 season. In the group are, back row, left to right: G. Britton, S. Britton, G. Bright. Second row: J. Henshaw (President), J. West, A. Bane, G.E. Britton, E.C. Craymer, A. Bowler, W. Baker. Third row: G.B. Britton (Treasurer), A. Bryant, F. Maggs (V. Capt), G.F. Fowler (Capt), W.S. Weight (Hon. Sec.). Front: A. Britton (scorer), J. Edwards, J.W. Nettle (umpire).

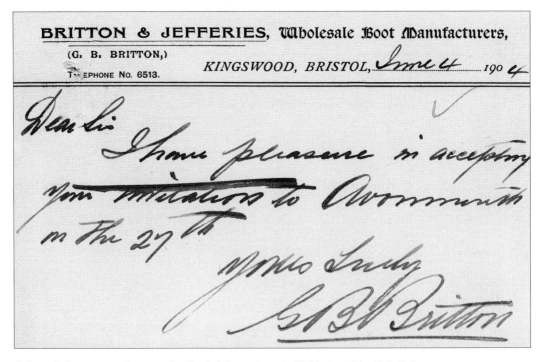

Acknowledgement card sent to the Docks' Committee in 1904, signed by G.B. Britton.

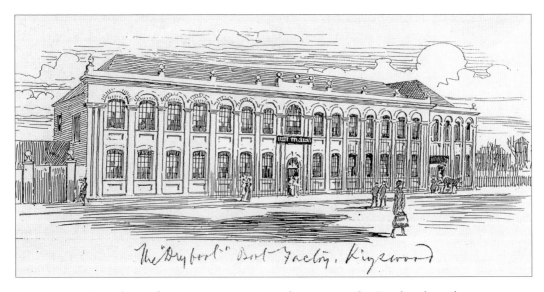

G.B. Britton Ltd, or The Dryfoot Boot Factory as it was known, in Lodge Road, as drawn by Loxton.

Above: Memoriam card for Handel Cossham, who died in 1890.

Left: Handel Cossham.

Cossham Memorial Hospital was built with money left in trust from the estate of Handel Cossham, first MP for Bristol East and local colliery owner, 'that I may hereafter be remembered by the sick and suffering as a friend who in death as well as in life has felt it his duty to try and lessen human suffering and increase human happiness'.

The hospital, designed by architect Mr F. Bligh-Bond and built by A.J. Beaven and Cowlin & Sons, cost £30,000 including furnishings and the laying out of the grounds.

The hospital was built using the most up-to-date methods, for example 'all angles were rounded and the junctions of wall and floor curved to prevent the lodgement of germs'. Bricks from the Hollybrook Brick Company were used along with locally quarried stone.

The turret clock which shows the time on four, 6ft diameter illuminated dials, is a fine example of the clockmaker's art. The clock was built to keep time to within two seconds per week, chimed the quarters on four silver-toned bells and struck the hour on a rich tenor.

The clock also had an automatic arrangement for illuminating the dials at sunset and an electronic arrangement that controlled and ran all of the clocks in the entire hospital. The clock was made by Kemp Brothers of Union Street.

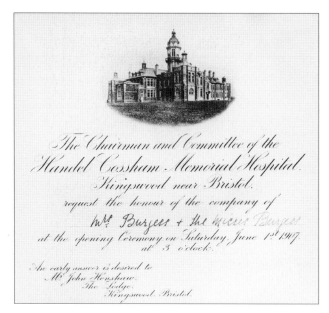

Left: Invitation to the opening ceremony at Cossham Hospital, 1 June 1907.

Below: The hospital was opened on 1 June 1907 by Mr Augustine Birrell MP. The Kingswood Evangel Band played a selection of music and tea was served to those present at the ceremony. The general public were admitted at 5 o'clock and it is estimated that 50,000 people inspected the building that evening.

Opposite, top: The operating table was one of the most modern fittings in the hospital and had been designed especially for Cossham Hospital by the surgical staff. It was made throughout of steel tubing, nickel plated and allowed tilting, rotating and raising entirely by foot levers so that no hand needed to touch the table itself. It was supported by a gunmetal piston rod which was embedded in a cylinder in the theatre floor. The table was raised and lowered by water pressure. It is 'of special satisfaction to note that this unique table was not only made in England but actually in Kingswood itself'. The cost of this table was seventy guineas.

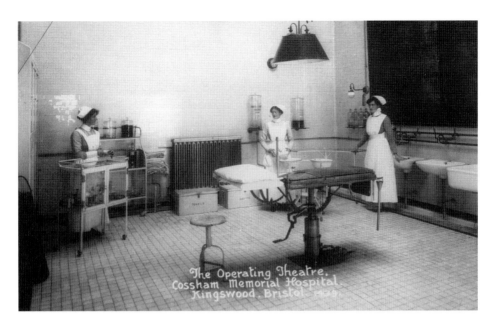

The Operating Theatre.
Cossham Memorial Hospital.
Kingswood. Bristol.

Within seven years of its opening, Cossham Hospital became one of the first Bristol hospitals to be used by the Red Cross as a war hospital. Hundreds of injured soldiers from the First World War were to pass through its wards.

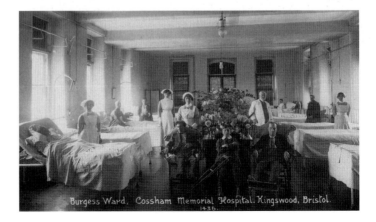

Burgess Ward, Cossham Memorial Hospital. Kingswood, Bristol.
1436.

Burgess Ward, Cossham Hospital, *c.* 1920.

Above and left: Cossham Hospital Carnival 1922, a fund-raising event where fancy dress was the order of the day. The soldier and the man on the horse are standing in the field where Kingswood Court nursing home now stands. Soundwell Road is in the background and the Bird in Hand off-licence can also be seen.

Below: Harvest Festival at Cossham Hospital, *c.* 1925.

Kingswood Castle. Little is known of the true origin of the tower which formed part of Kingswood Castle. It would appear that at some point in its history it had been used as a windmill for grinding corn but prior to this it could well have been part of Captain Copleys works, where an attempt was made to smelt iron using Kingswood coal. Excavations on the site in the 1960s, then owned by Bristol Water Works, revealed ashes from furnaces which existed here long ago. The tower itself is believed to have dated from the mid-seventeenth century and is thought to be the blast tower used by Captain Copley. He was assisted by Dud Dudley, who had patented a new smelting process in Warwickshire and had begun to prosper, but the local iron master became jealous and attacked and destroyed his works. Following the Civil War, Dudley came to Bristol and made the aquaintance of Captain Copley. There are conflicting reports but it is said that here at Kingswood, Dudley's process was successful, but once again he fell foul of the iron masters, this time from Bristol, and they brought about his downfall. He lost heart and died in poverty but he had laid the foundations of Britain's iron trade and the use of coal to smelt iron. His process died with him and was not used again until 1713 when Abraham Darby used it at Coalbrookdale. By the late 1800s, the then owner of the site, Mr Craymer, had built a castellated house adjoining the tower.

Braines' History of Kingswood Forest tells us that:

'… in the basement of the tower there is a circular room, 18ft in diameter; walls 4ft thick. The tower is 55ft high. The mantelpiece of the drawing room and cornice are of carved oak taken from Bristol Cathedral during its restoration. The centrepiece of the mantel is from the Duke of Malborough's house and contains a coat of arms. It was purchased from Mr Munro, Bristol. The top part is the old pulpit front of the cathedral. There is an ancient chest from Fontel Abbey, an immense oak table and chair, very handsomely carved, taken from Bitton Church, a sideboard of carved oak with pillars – the ancient communion rails from Old Sodbury Church. A handsome oak bedstead on which Queen Elizabeth slept at the 'Fourteen Stars' at Counterslip. A little cot, childs, five hundred years old. The house looked like a miniature Windsor Castle.'

Above: During 1969 thousands of tons of concrete were pumped into the ground at Hopewell Hill to make a two million gallon reservoir for the Kingswood area. The reservoir is divided into two chambers, with forty concrete columns supporting the roof. It cost a total of £100,000. This picture shows Mr W.F. Small, assistant divisional engineer standing in the new reservoir.

Above, right: The sign from the gate of Lodge Hill reservoir, which stood on the site between Lodgeside and Cossham Hospital. This area has been built on during 2003/04 but the reservoir itself has been retained as an underground car park.

Opposite, above: The original water tower, pumping station and reservoir at Hopewell Hill, Kingswood, *c.* 1900. Demolished in the 1950s, this tower stood behind the waterworks' offices which were where the Kingswood Court Nursing Home stands today. To the left of the picture are some steps cut into the bank of the second reservoir which is shown below.

Opposite, below: Kingswood Castle overlooking the reservoir, *c.* 1900. This large reservoir is still extant and is used as a storage yard. The water tower of Lodge Hill Reservoir is just visible in the background to the left of the castle. Early in 1940 the reservoir was covered for the first time and during the first raid on Bristol, a bomb dropped through the roof. The damage was soon repaired and the flat roof became the perfect place for a tennis court.

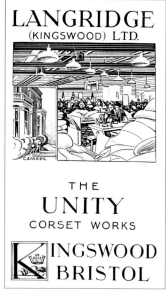

Langridges Corset Factory in Kingswood started production in 1921 with four girls and Mr Ryall as manager. By 1932 no less than 250 workers staffed two factories.

The name Langridge is associated with the early history of corset making. Around 1830 Mr Langridge started business in Totterdown. He made very exclusive corsets which were worked with hand-embroidered designs in silk. Eventually he moved his business to Temple Street where he manufactured crinolines, for which he has the reputation of being the pioneer. Original Langridge products bear the 'Unity' trademark. Early corsetry was very rigid, often consisting of at least sixty separate pieces of material. Whalebone was used for reinforcement and the most popular colours were dove grey and black. Whalebone supports were eventually replaced by steels.

The business was acquired by Mr E. Sheriff in 1894 and a move was made to St George. Later Mr Sheriff teamed up with Mr S.D. Ryall, who became managing director and the two decided to build an up-to-date factory for the making of better-class goods under the style of Langridge (Kingswood) Ltd. They exhibited at the British Trade and Industries Fair in 1923, causing considerable interest with the introduction of Celanese satin in a range of five colours.

The factory on Two Mile Hill was small, but up to date, although the only heating was from a single stove on the ground floor, whose chimney served to heat the upper floor! Within ten years of opening there had been four extensions to the factory, covering the whole of the available site. Additional premises in Waters Road, known as the leather factory, were bought in 1930 as the business expanded. During the Second World War, only one of the three sites was allowed to continue making corsetry. The other two were used for the manufacture of parachutes and uniforms. When Mr Ryall died in 1940, his son, Charles, became chairman. The factory was honoured in 1943 by the visit on 14 July of Her Majesty Queen Mary. The original building on Two Mile Hill was sold in 1952 as the Waters Road site was extended. The name of the company had changed to Unity Corset Factories and Fantasie Foundations had been established as the marketing company. The business grew rapidly after the war with a London showroom established in Grosvenor Street in 1953.

Mr S.D. Ryall, managing director.

In the early days, the cutters were nearly always men. With unerring eye and steady hand they would guide the long, razor sharp knives along the lines of the design. The pieces for the finished garment were bundled together, placed in a basket and taken to the machine room where they were stitched together.

The machinists, all women, sat at long benches; speed and accuracy were essential. In the machine room, the corset went from one machine to another, each time gaining in strength and shape. Eventually hooks and eyes and suspenders were added and the whole garment trimmed and inspected before being sent for packaging.

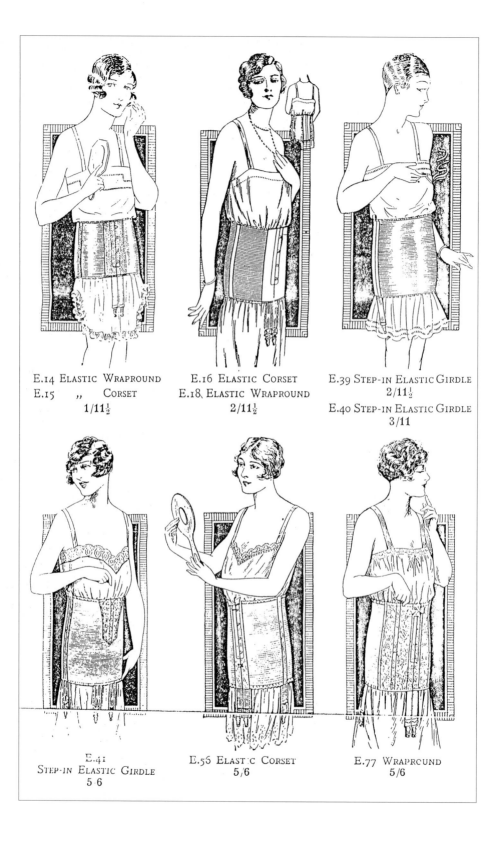

E.14 ELASTIC WRAPROUND
E.15   „   CORSET
1/11½

E.16 ELASTIC CORSET
E.18 ELASTIC WRAPROUND
2/11½

E.39 STEP-IN ELASTIC GIRDLE
2/11½
E.40 STEP-IN ELASTIC GIRDLE
3/11

E.41
STEP-IN ELASTIC GIRDLE
5·6

E.56 ELASTIC CORSET
5/6

E.77 WRAPROUND
5/6

Langridge Ltd (Kingswood), annual outing, 1924, taken outside Zion Sunday School in Grantham Road. The charabanc belonged to the Silver Queen Motor Company of No. 321 Two Mile Hill.

Above and right: A postcard and advertisement for the Fantasie factory from the 1970s.

There's a special place for you at
FANTASIE

Fantasie girls refuse to be just part of the crowd. Each one stands out as a real person. They're quickly taught to be an expert machinist. They become part of a specialist team.

The work is interesting, the pay good—and it gets better! For example, start at 15 and there's a guaranteed rise every six months until you're 18. Piecework opportunities, bonuses, plus plentiful opportunities for promotion.

Training courses—with pay—are available to girls of 15 and 16. Have a chat with Miss Marion Mercer, our Personnel Manageress She'll tell you about the hours, rates of pay, and anything else you want to know.

Call or 'phone.

FANTASIE
FOUNDATIONS
LTD.

*Waters Road,
Kingswood,
Bristol
BS15 2ED.*

Tel. 671871

Opposite: Corset designs from the late 1920s.

Zion Free Methodist Chapel. Wesleyan Methodism in Kingswood in the 1840s was very strong, but by 1849 a split had occurred and some members formed a separate group – the Wesleyan Reform Movement. With no building of their own, the group met in local cottages. Two Sunday Schools were formed, one in a loft in Lewtons Lane, later known as Factory Lane and the other at Two Mile Hill in what was then the schoolroom built by Robert Charleton (now part of Latham Autos).

The present church was opened on 22 June 1854 at a cost of £2,150. It seated 750 and had school accommodation for 400. It is said that the land on which the church stands was owned by a Mr Robert Churchill, who refused to sell the land to church trustees. A friend of the church bought the land and resold it to church trustees. It is said that the deal took place in The Black Horse public house. The congregation gave generously, some giving their labour, digging foundations, hauling stone as well as giving money. Five years later, in 1859, schoolrooms were added and in 1860 side galleries were built, paid for by Daniel Flook. In 1897, the Sunday School had 1,332 names on its books.

Opposite, above: The chapel interior, *c.* 1950.

Opposite, centre: In 1912 a new schoolroom was built in Grantham Road, the old schoolroom being used as the minister's vestry, the organ room and choir vestry. A huge hole was made in the north wall of the chapel and a fine organ loft and choir gallery were built (see top photograph). The foundation stone was laid by W.H. Butler. This photograph shows the crowds at the stone-laying ceremony in 1912.

Opposite, below: The opening of Zion United Methodist schoolroom in Grantham Road, 1913.

The new schoolroom in Grantham Road, *c.* 1913. This magnificent building was demolished in 1987 and flats were built on the site.

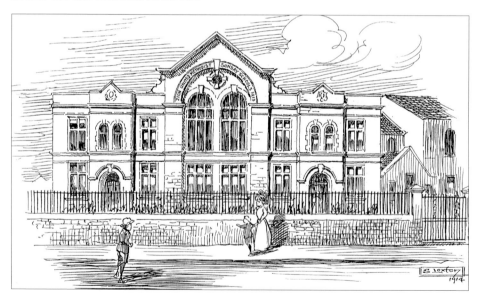

The schoolroom as seen by Loxton, *c.* 1914.

Opposite, above: The interior of the schoolroom, *c.* 1913. My father, Bill (Don) Payne, was one of a number of small boys who hand-pumped this organ for Sunday school services.

Preachers of the Methodist Free Churches in the Kingswood Circuit, June 1872. From left to right, back row: W. Williams, E. Clark, J. Wynes, H. Wilshire, J. Godfrey, W. Wilshire, T. Edwards, J. Moss, G. Bateman, B. Bird, W. Vowles. Third row: J. Lovell, W. Davis, J. Roberts, I. White, A.P. Monks, C.J. Tyler, D. Elbrow, J. Bateman. Second row: J. Burgess, I. Britton, S. Britton, W. Hulbert, Mr Whitchurch, S. Green, T. Gully, W. Butler, J. Martin, S. Ollis. Front row: G.F. Thompson, J. Warwick, T .Salter, J. Burgess Snr, G. Ollis, T. Rothwell, J. Brewer.

This very early photograph was taken outside Zion United Methodist Chapel by A. Summers of Kingswood.

Opposite, above: The newly refurbished Kingswood Methodist Church about to be opened by Mr W. Round, Revd Joyce Plumb and Mr and Mrs M. Alderson. The church itself has been restructured, the last service in the original building being held on 23 August 1987. The facelift cost a total of £250,000 and the new church was rededicated and reopened by Cllr Marmaduke Alderson, Lord Mayor of Bristol, on 30 April 1988. The galleries have now gone, to be replaced by a first-floor worship area and the ground floor is used as a meeting place for various organisations. Unfortunately the original stone tablet inscribed 'Zion Free Methodist Chapel' was obliterated when the church was renamed.

Above: Zion War Memorial. At the outbreak of war in 1914, a 'Boys Rememberance Society' was formed and at regular intervals, parcels and letters were sent to 'our boys at the Front'. Every Sunday afternoon, hymn No. 549 in the Sunday school hymnal was movingly sung by scholars and teachers alike, 'From homes of quiet peace we lift up hands of prayer'.

Twenty-four of those from the church who went to fight did not return. A memorial was erected in the churchyard. It bears the inscription:

In ever grateful memory of the men of this church and school who gave their lives in the Great War 1914 – 1919 and in grateful recognition of those who served and safely returned.

The following names are listed on the memorial: Lt A.D. Anderson, Pt W. Alvis, Pt W. Britton, Pt. W. Bright, Pt G. Bateman, Pt G. Barrington, Pt W. Bryant, Seaman E. Clark, Pt R. Clark, Pt G. Clark, Pt E. Demmery, Pt E. Gay, Pt. W. Howes, Pt J. Haskins, Pt W. Pearce, Sgt J. Paget, Pt C. Plaster, Pt T. Palmer, Pt G. Shattock, Pt F. Sims, Pt E.W. Tanner, Pt E.M. Tanner, Sap. C.G. Warne, Gun. C. Wright.

On 3 September 1939, the devastating news that war had broken out again was announced from the rostrum during morning worship. A 'Comfort Committee' was formed as in 1914, as many of Zion's men and women were called up. Four of them did not return and their names were duly added to the war memorial: Sgt C.R. Bateman, Gun. P. Lowman, Pt R. Pearce, Pt W. Wilkins.

Bristol boundary signs – then and now. A red circle on a white column once stood outside the Black Horse on the corner of Blackhorse Road (left) – seen here in around 1968. The present sign looks like this (right).

VIEW OF INTENDED WESLEYAN METHODIST CHAPEL KINGSWOOD

Above: Samuel Budgett.

Above, right: The Wesleyan Chapel, Blackhorse Road, was built in 1843 for Wesleyan Methodists, largely due to the energies of Samuel Budgett. He said that he 'would have it and have it free from debt'. He begged money from Bristol and Bath and from as far afield as Liverpool and London. For his last fundraising effort he suggested that they have a 'great gathering'. Mr Daniel Flook proposed that people were brought out from Bristol and given tea for the sum of one shilling. This was done and 'tea' was provided for 1,200 people. When the accounts were read, to everyone's surprise, the chapel was out of debt and had £26 in hand towards building a new schoolroom.

The chapel was large and airy with galleries around three sides, painted with white and gold. Ornamental gasaliers hung from them. It could seat approximately 1,000 people in box pews that were topped with polished mahogany.

Samuel Budgett is buried here. His funeral on 7 May 1851 was a huge event in Kingswood, with crowds following the coffin and lining the route. The *Bristol Times* of that week paid tribute: 'Rarely has a neighbourhood suffered a greater loss in the death of a man, than Kingswood in the decease of Mr Budgett, whose charity was unbounded and who distributed with discrimination and liberality and without ostentation, fully £2,000 a year from his own pocket.'

Behind the chapel, and built in the same style, is the day school, erected with Mr Budgett's help at a cost of £800 and behind this is the infant school.

The chapel has recently been the victim of arsonists, with a fierce blaze in July 2004, leaving the building completely gutted.

Above: Kingswood Wesleyan Chapel, 1980.

Left: The graveyard at the Wesleyan Chapel, although now very overgrown, has many ornate gravestones including this monument to Samuel Pullin and his family. Mr Pullin was well known in the district. The story goes that he was a carpenter by trade and made his own coffin which he kept in the hallway of his house for many years. He was also known for wearing a dark-green top hat!

Top: The shop belonging to Thomas Critchley which stood on the corner of Blackhorse Road, 1981.

Centre: Claremont Place at No. 377-9 Two Mile Hill and R.Z. Hopes wool shop at number No. 381, *c.* 1967.

Below: Claremont Place, 2004.

two

Regent Street and Around

Regent Street, Kingswood, *c.* 1912. On the left is the YMCA hut which was destroyed by fire in the mid–1920s and to the right is the junction with South Road.

The YMCA hut, Kingswood, as drawn by Loxton, *c.* 1920.

The local policeman poses for the camera outside the YMCA hut, Regent Street.

The interior of the YMCA hut showing the reading room, drawn by Loxton, c. 1920.

Kingswood YMCA, AFC Champions 1918/19.

Silver Craig, South Road, *c.* 1966. Once the home of Dr Ian MacDonald it was demolished to make way for Somerfield's car park.

Troy House, No. 36 South Road, *c.* 1966. Once a doctor's surgery, it is now demolished

Tower House, No. 69 South Road, *c.* 1927.

Right: J. Moon, ironmonger, at the junction of South Road and Regent Street, *c.* 1910. Moon's later became a confectioner and tobacconist shop. Graham Bamford took children there from Band of Hope meetings at Zion Chapel to buy sweets in the 1930s.

Below: This is Regent Street in around 1953 and the shop on the left with the clock, just past the Kingswood boundary sign, is the Dairy Café. The café was owned by the Hoddinott family who also sold ice cream from the side window of their house in Talbot Avenue.

Joseph Adolphus Zahringer came to England from the Black Forest area of Germany in the 1870s to learn the watchmaking trade. He was apprenticed to a maker in Wotton-Under-Edge, Gloucestershire, before moving to Kingswood. He opened a small shop on the corner of Boultons Lane before moving to the present premises in Regent Street. Joseph married a local girl, Thirza Denning, whose family came from Cockroad. He died in 1933 at the age of sixty-two and a large crowd gathered for his funeral. He was a much loved and respected man. Thirza ran the shop through the war years, her son Cecil, who was working at the Douglas factory, helping her when he could. After the war, her youngest son Reginald and his wife, Audrey, helped Cecil to run the business. Thirza died in the 1950s. Cecil was much more interested in music than clocks. He had played the piano in local cinemas during the silent film era and following that he played the dance halls with the popular Regent Dance Band. Cecil died in the late 1970s leaving the business to Reginald, Audrey and their family. Their sons still run the business today.

G.A. Owen, at No. 10 Regent Street, was owned from 1961 by Cecil Gapper. Cecil went into the butchery trade at fourteen, training at the Cheltenham Road branch of the Co-op, before moving to the Clouds Hill branch as a manager. He also worked at the Danish Bacon Company before working for George Owen at Regent Street, taking over the business when Mr Owen retired. Meat was bought from the Old Market Street meat markets, such as Borthwick's, and in Mr Owen's time was often brought back to Regent Street on the next available tram! In later years the meat was bought from a Nailsea slaughterhouse. In 1976 Cecil's son, David, came into the business, running the shop until it finally closed in 1996. However, things could have been very different: Cecil was a promising footballer and was capped for Bristol Boys and had trials for Bristol Rovers until rheumatic fever at the age of thirteen put an end to his football career.

Above: Cecil Gapper seen here in the shop.

Right: David Gapper, seen here in the shop, had the butchery trade in his blood from an early age. Here (right) in 1965, he is in his butcher's apron with Ted Stallard, Cecil's assistant for many years.

Above and below: The Regent Garage stood at the end of York Terrace and was both a petrol station and repair garage and also an official agent for Ford, *c.* 1954.

The Picture House, Kingswood, Bristol 36

Kingswood was one of the first Bristol suburbs to have a cinema. The Regent Cinema opened in 1912. Silent films were shown and a pianist would sit at the front and play along with the film. Mr Kear was the manager. He was a little man, who would stand on a chair at the front and wave his arms asking the audience to 'Be quiet please'. He would often be answered with a shower of peanut shells. Winkles were another favourite thing to eat at the Regent. Taken from their shells with a pin, the empty shells were often thrown at the screen if the film was not up to standard. There was a '2d rush' on Saturday afternoons, a first-come, first-served event mainly for children. The cinema closed in 1949. A Be Wise shop now stands on the site.

Regent Picture House

REGENT ST., KINGSWOOD, BRISTOL

*Continuous Performances Nightly
From 6.30. Children's Matinee Saturday at 2. Evening 5.30 to 10.30.*

VISIT THE REGENT PICTURE HOUSE
THE KINEMA THAT ALWAYS GIVES FULL VALUE

Right: The Regent Cinema by Loxton.

Regent Street, *c*. 1907. The houses on the right are on the corner of Downend Road.

Downend Road, 1966, showing Boultons Road on the left. The large brick building left of centre is David Williams Corset Factory, founded in 1867. The shopping centre car park now covers the whole of this site.

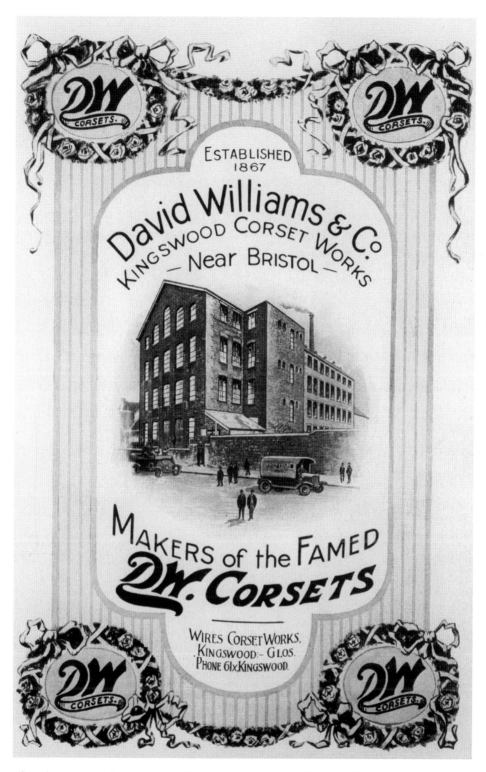

This advertisement from around 1913 shows the factory in Downend Road.

Regent Street at its junction with Downend Road, *c.* 1905. Dr Grace's surgery is the dark, square building in the centre of the picture. The double-fronted house to its left is Dr Perrott's house which was demolished for the building of the Ambassador Cinema in the 1930s.

The Ambassador Cinema was opened by Captain Sir D.W. Gunston MCMP on 26 March 1938. The building's main feature was its tower which was lit with red and blue neon lights and its stairway had a stained-glass window commemorating W.G. Grace. In December 1940 the Ambassador lost its roof during the Blitz. A mine exploded at the back of the building causing a sales girl to be blown clean out of the cinema itself and into the foyer. The entire audience sheltered under the Circle and fortunately no one was seriously hurt. Also during the war years a British Restaurant was opened in the Ambassador as part of a government scheme to keep the population fed but it wasn't well supported and never really viable.

Above: The Ambassador Café was situated above the foyer. It was accessible from the cinema or direct from Regent Street and was decorated in true 1930s style. It also had a maple dance floor.

Opposite, below: Dr Charles J. Perrott's house on Regent Street, which was next to his surgery. When the YMCA hut was burnt down in the 1920s, Dr Perrott allowed his house to be used for YMCA purposes. He was president of the Kingswood branch from 1929. Charles Perrott came from Dublin and was Medical Officer of Health for Kingswood from 1894 until his death in 1936. He had been a respected physician and surgeon in the district for upwards of fifty years, starting work as Dr Henry Grace's assistant. He was also church warden at Holy Trinity Church for many years.

The auditorium of the Ambassador seated almost 2,000 people. The décor was beige and dark blue with hundreds of lights sunk into the ceiling.

Just after the Second World War the Ambassador was renamed the Odeon. This publicity shot is for Brains' pies and sausages and dates from the late 1940s.

Regent Street in the late 1940s showing the bomb damage to the cinema and Dr Grace's surgery (in the centre of the picture, at this time called Shipsides) and also Woolworths and Jones' department store on the opposite side of the road.

Right: The Odeon Cinema 1953, decorated for the Coronation and the showing of *A Queen is Crowned*.

Below: The Odeon Cinema in a picture from the late 1950s. It closed on 11 March 1961 and was bought out by the Rank Organisation for conversion into a ten pin bowling alley.

The Odeon was stripped of its red and gold plasterwork and the massive sloping balcony to leave just a shell. It was converted into a two-floor, twenty-four-lane bowling alley at a cost of £250,000. The 63ft-long lanes were made edgeways, built up by adding tiers of tongued maple until the necessary width was obtained. When placed flat upon their supporting beams, the alleys were then sanded, lacquered and finally wax polished. A total of 50 tons of timber was used in the construction.

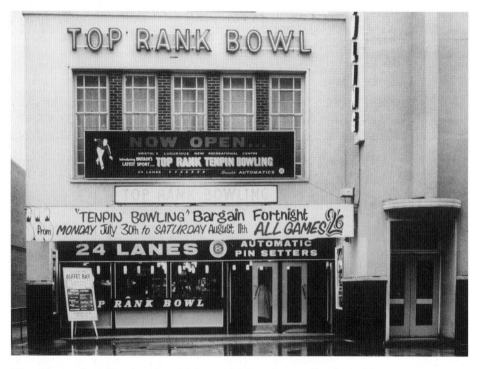

The alley was formally opened on 28 August 1961 and opened to the public on 25 September 1961 from 10.00 a.m. to midnight, opening an hour earlier at weekends. The first bowl was bowled by starlet Yvonne Buckingham. More than 2,000 people visited the 'Kingswood Bowl' on the first day and during the evening there was often a waiting time of two or three hours, even with all twenty-four lanes in play.

A Harp Lager League Match.

Above, left: The Milkmaid Milk Bar.

Above, right: Norman Wisdom visits the Top Rank Bowl, 20 January 1962.

An advert from December 1962.

Kingswood ladies at the bowling alley.

The bowling alley, boarded up, just prior to its demolition in 1973 to make way for the new shopping centre.

Dr Grace's surgery (centre) in the 1960s. This historic building was demolished to make way for the new shopping centre. Dr Henry Grace was the eldest of the Grace brothers, who were famous for their ability as both doctors and cricketers. There was a walkway through this building, in the 1960s, that housed an aquarium. I remember as a child walking through, hoping that my mum would be there at the other end when I came out. There were also some stairs that led to a first floor meeting room, though when young I never dared venture up them. In the 1940s this was the meeting place of the Young Communist League.

Pictures from the 1970s showing, on the left, Dr Grace's surgery, Price-Sigrist the chemist, Lutons bakery, the Midland Bank and Widger's wallpaper shop. Further along the road, Brook's dry cleaners, Rogers & Harris' fruit and veg shop and the Bunch of Grapes off-licence. The lane to the side was known as John Garrs Alley and ran down to the bottom of London Street. In the 1930s there was a slaughterhouse about half-way down on the bend in the lane. The animals would be herded down from Regent Street and a large gate would be opened out across the lane to stop the animals from running straight down it and out into London Street.

Left: Victoria Buildings at the junction of Regent Street and Halls Road, *c.* 1900. This was the first office of the West Gloucestershire Water Company. The company was formed in 1884 and remained responsible for the district's water supply for seventy-five years, until it was taken over by Bristol Water Works in 1959 as part of a government regrouping scheme.

Below: Regent Street, *c.* 1905. Dr Grace's surgery can be seen on the left and the SWASH store, the forerunner of Woolworths, is on the right.

Regent Street.

Above and below: The Civic Electrical Store on the opposite corner of Halls Road to Victoria buildings. Harry Worth did a famous series of television advertisements for this company. He features in both of these photographs.

Regent Street in the late 1940s. The Don, otherwise known as Parkers faggot and peas shop, is to the left.

Moravian Road showing the Esso garage, c. 1968. This picture was taken just a few yards from the junction with Regent Street.

Corona mineral waters delivery vehicles with staff, Wood Road, Kingswood.

"Kingswood Queen" Motor Coaches

Copy.

PROPRIETORS:
G FELTHAM & SONS LTD

DIRECTORS
W. FELTHAM
R. FELTHAM
A. FELTHAM

MOTOR COACH PROPRIETORS
AND HAULAGE CONTRACTORS

BRISTOL
TELEPHONE :

AND 54 MORAVIAN ROAD, KINGSWOOD
BRISTOL
TELEPHONE 7-4827/8

Top and above left and right: Feltham's Coaches (Kingswood Queen) was started by a woman – Harriet Feltham (above left), *née* Leonard, who lived in a little cottage in Potters Wood. She came from a family of hauliers and when her husband George died in 1883, at the young age of forty-six, leaving her with four young children, she had to find a way of providing for them. She started to chop wood and sell it from a homemade hand cart. Then she bought a donkey and used it to carry coal from the pit and sold both coal and 'stick'. Later, she bought a pony and cart and one of her sons, Gilbert, stayed home from school to help her. The business developed and they bought a bigger horse and cart and a wagonette, which was how the passenger business started. The company was named G. Feltham and expanded to include wedding-hire and funerals as well as outings. Walter Feltham, son of Gilbert, told of how his father bought a Ford fourteen-seater at a cost of £800, a small fortune in those days. When it was delivered, Walter practised driving it for two hours and the next day took the coach full of passengers to Weston-Super-Mare.

Right: When war broke out in 1939, the government commandeered the best vehicles for military use. The war years were hard but when the war was over, day trips and holidays began again and the business went from strength to strength. In 1947, the nationalisation of the haulage business was a big blow to the firm. The three directors, Walter, Reginald and Albert Feltham, all grandsons of Harriet, decided to concentrate on the passenger side of the business. In 1955 the company opened a new coach station in Moravian Road with a large garage behind it. It had its own petrol pumps, a modern office block and waiting room facilities for thirty-five passengers. There were over thirty pick-up points and offices around Bristol with a fleet of twenty-four coaches painted in the blue and yellow livery that became a familiar sight on the streets of Kingswood. The business was eventually sold to Wessex Coaches, who took over on 1 January 1960.

KINGSWOOD QUEEN MOTOR COACHES
Props.: G. FELTHAM & SONS LTD.

Let us quote you for your outings
ANYTHING · ANYTIME · ANYWHERE
Distance no object—Any number catered for

DAILY EXCURSIONS TO ALL THE POPULAR RESORTS

HOLIDAY PERIOD BOOKINGS TO

Teignmouth, Torquay, Paignton, Bournemouth, Weymouth, Southsea, Seaton, Sidmouth, Exmouth, Brighton

BOOKING OFFICES —
99, STAPLE HILL ROAD, FISHPONDS	Phone 53239
82, MORAVIAN ROAD, KINGSWOOD	Phone 73581
YOUNGS, NEWSAGENT, DOWNEND	Phone 55320
BUSHELLS, NEWSAGENT, OLDBURY COURT	Phone 52305
MARTINS STORES, HILLSIDE ROAD, ST. GEORGE ...	Phone 73488
SPIRES, 317, TWO MILE HILL ROAD, KINGSWOOD ...	Phone 73566
WHITTOCK, STANLEY ROAD, WARMLEY	Phone 74193
COMER, MENDIP VIEW, WICK	Phone Abson 200

Opposite above: Harriet Feltham's cottage at the junction of Moravian Road and Hanham Road, *c.* 1907. The sign on the cottage reads: 'Brakes, wagonettes, landaus, traps to hire'. In the background, to the left is Pow's Boot factory. Behind the cottage was the slaughterhouse of Mrs Short. On Fridays, pigs would be herded along Hanham Road to be slaughtered. Straw was laid to soak up the blood and then set alight. In the 1930s there were twenty-one slaughterhouses in Kingswood district. Most were connected to family butchering businesses but two were wholesale butchers where a good deal of slaughtering took place for the Bristol meat markets. From 1934, all slaughter men had to be licensed under the Slaughter of Animals Act which also required mechanical stunning of animals before sticking. The poleaxe for cows was also outlawed at this time.

Opposite below: Reg Feltham with his coach taken outside Potterswood Tin Mission in Moravian Road, *c.* 1930

Potters Wood Methodist Church, or the Old Tin Mission as it was known, was transported to Moravian Road from Keynsham in 1892. The building itself cost £25, with the transportation costing 13s. It cost a further £8 15s 0d to dismantle and re-erect it. In 1944, following his purchase of Pow's Boot Factory, an offer was made by Mr Lucas to purchase the site of the chapel for the extension of his factory. The church declined but, after much deliberation, the site was eventually exchanged with M. Lucas for land and a new building at Pows Road. Elbrow's were employed to build the new chapel and work began in 1956. The new chapel was officially opened by Mrs H.P. Lucas on 17 August 1957, the congregation marching from the old chapel to the new building along Moravian Road with the Bristol East Temperance Band in attendance.

The board of Douglas motorcycles, *c.* 1910. William Douglas and his brother Edwin came to Bristol from Greenock. They set up in business together and bought a small forge and in 1882 Douglas Engineering was born. Within a few years they had a foundry in Hanham Road and for about twenty years they supplied the boot and shoe industry with lasts and castings, made lamp posts, manhole covers and drain gratings which can still be seen today. Edwin eventually left the business and in 1907 William Douglas made an association with J.J. Barter and produced the first Douglas motorcycle.

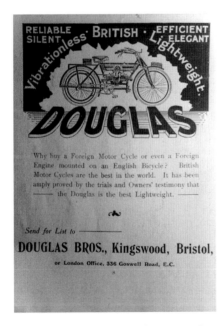

Above Left: An advertisement from around 1910.

Above Right: Local Kingswood man Harry Bamford on his Douglas motorcycle during the First World War. This is one of a series of twenty postcards produced showing Douglas motorcycles and their riders. Some 25,000 of these despatch bikes were produced by the factory.

An early Douglas Motors delivery vehicle registered in 1904.

A North American serviceman on a Douglas 4hp motorcycle with sidecar, which would have been painted khaki green for military use during the First World War.

Above left: During the First World War, many women were employed in the factory. This picture shows a lathe and its operator standing on wooden slats known as duck boards to keep the cold from her feet. These slats became impregnated with oil over time, which was a huge problem when there was a fire at the works in 1927.

Above right: After the First World War, many military motorcycles were returned to the factory to be reconditioned for re-sale. Any soldier who had ridden a 'Duggie' at the Front wanted one of his own once de-mobbed. They were usually painted black and this model has 'sit up and beg' handle bars.

A Douglas 500cc prototype motorcycle from the mid-1950s.

Her Majesty Queen Mary visiting the Douglas works in 1941, when production in the factory was mainly for the Ministry of Aircraft Production. Queen Mary's sons, Prince Albert, (later George VI) and Prince Edward (later Edward VIII) both bought Douglas motorcycles during the 1920s.

Australian, Billy Conoulty, on an OB model road racing bike, with Mr S.L. Bailey and mechanic George Olds after winning the 'Gold Helmet Trophy.' Mr Olds was the owner of a garage in Laurel Street, Kingswood.

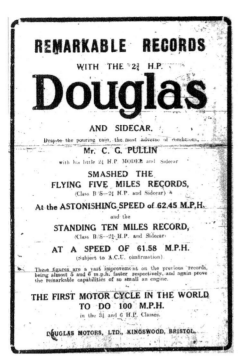

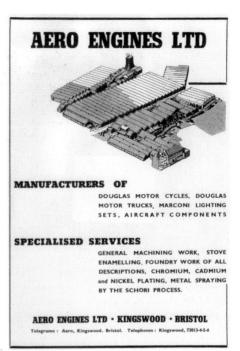

Douglas advertisements from around 1922 (left) and 1938 (right).

A two-storey Douglas Vespa delivery lorry, *c.* 1955.

Douglas owned a sports ground adjacent to the factory in Wood Road. During the war years, Bristol Rovers played there. It was also the venue for many charity football matches in the 1960s and also saw the likes of Olympic Runner Diane Leather and cyclist Reg Harris compete there. During the late 1950s and '60s, as above, it was the venue for the Kingswood schools sports events.

Barry Russell on a 1930 600cc Douglas S6 with John Lewis, Mayor of Kingswood, in the side car and Raymond Cordy on a 2¾ Douglas motorcycle for the inauguration of the Kingswood Heritage Trail, April 1990. The trail was launched to celebrate the centenary of the foundation of the Kingswood Urban Board.

Regent Street, *c.* 1905. The Golden Hart pub is to the left, licenced at that time to Isaac Bryant. The junction of Moravian Road is further into the picture on the left, just past the tram pole.

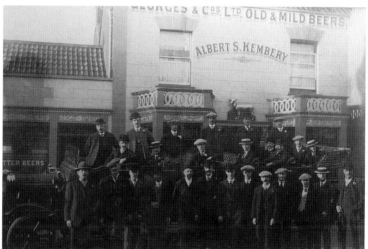

A 1920s photograph of the annual Golden Hart outing to North Wraxall to gather nuts. Every October, the pub regulars would arrange this outing, collecting 'cobb' or hazelnuts in hessian nail-bags. On the way back they would stop for a drink at The Crown at Marshfield. The Golden Hart was at this time licensed to Albert S. Kembery.

The Golden Hart with the National Provincial Bank on the corner of Moravian Road *c.* 1968. These buildings were demolished around 1970.

Graham Bamford at No. 67 Regent Street in 1928. The business was originally
opened around 1840 by Edward Haskins and Edward James Bamford bought
the business in 1896, his son Graham coming to work in the shop in 1925.
Edward died in 1945 and Graham took over until the shop closed in 1977
following a compulsory purchase order. The interior of the shop was amazing.
How Graham found anything was a mystery, but he seemed to know where
everything was. You could buy anything – one nail or screw, a single washer or
curtain ring, a garden fork, bucket, string, oil, paraffin – anything. In his father's
day there was a small forge in the back of the shop where Mr Bamford would
make you up a toasting fork or repair the handle of your garden trowel while
you waited. The building was demolished to make way for the Chase Inn.

Graham and Elsie Bamford with Raymond Cordy, 1977.

Every inch of space was used and everything was labelled in Graham's own distinctive handwriting and every box tied up with string.

Graham's scales and work bench.

Graham and Elsie Bamford behind the counter. The box in front of Graham reads 'Sovereign saw-edged bread knives 50p each'.

Regent Street showing the Clock Tower, *c.* 1918. To the left of the picture is Henry J. Flook's, provision and tea dealer, and the Bijou Bazaar. The little boy leaning on the lamp post is Graham Bamford.

In November 1897 Kingswood District Council agreed an account of £20, the purchase price of the site in Regent Street upon which it was proposed to build a clock tower and public clock to commemorate the Diamond Jubilee of Her Majesty Queen Victoria. Eight of the council members voted for the building and three against, the chairman, W.D. Strange, being so strongly in favour of the memorial that it became known as Strange's Folly. It was intended to build the tower half as high again, with the extra costs being raised locally. The foundations for such a tower were laid but the money was not forthcoming.

In February 1888 the Clock Tower Committee purchased the site, which was originally part of the yard of The Golden Hart Inn, a condition of sale being that the tower be erected within twelve months. Public subscriptions totalled £266 19s 5d. The clock tower was built by Kingswood builder Mr Alfred Amos of Regent Street at a cost of £142 16s 0d, the plans being drawn up by Mr Mackay. The clock mechanism was supplied by Kemp Brothers of Union Street at a cost of £72 15s 0d, the weather vane at £1 0s 5d and the bronze plaque to Queen Victoria £6. The contract made provision for the best Cattybrook bricks to be used externally, the internal brickwork being from the Mount Hill Brickyard.

Mr F.H. Shipton of Downend, who was apprenticed to Mr Charles Kemp, was the clockmaker and Mr Edward Kemp personally supervised the castings and patterns which were made in Fairfax Street. There was concern that pedestrians walking under the clock tower might be crushed if the weights of the clock should fall and so the trunk of a newly felled tree was built into the platform below the 200lb weights, to prevent them from crashing into the street below in the event of part of the mechanism coming adrift. The clock pendulum was six feet long, the minute hand two feet six inches and the main wheels of the clock twelve inches in diameter and made of gunmetal. Each of the three dials is 4ft in diameter.

The Bristol side was replaced after being shattered in 1940 by the same bomb that hit the Ambassador Cinema. The clock was wound weekly by Kemp Brothers until 1951, when council workmen took over the task. Access was through a trapdoor in the platform, the room containing the mechanism being just seventy inches square. The clock is now electrically operated.

Regent Street showing the shops of G.A. Tayler, poulterer and purveyor, Peark's Stores and Kingswood County Drug Stores owned by the chemist, F. Moss, *c.* 1900.

The Moravian Church in Kingswood was founded in 1741 but the present building by Foster and Wood dates from 1856. Behind the church is a tiny burial ground which preserves memorial stones from the Moravian graveyard that was formerly in Upper Maudlin Street, Bristol. Behind the church is the manse, which is now an accountant's office.

In the grounds of the Moravian manse stood a mulberry tree, planted by the prolific hymn writer James Montgomery in 1845. He wrote amongst others, *Angels from the realms of Glory* and *Hail to the Lords Anointed*. The original tree fell in a storm in the 1980s but the present owners of the site have planted another in its place.

A group from the Moravian church, *c.* 1930.

Whitefield's
Tabernacle.
Congregational
Church. Kingswood.
The Old & New Buildings

Whitfield Tabernacle. Whitfield's meeting house in Park Road was completed in 1742 and it is probable that the building that stands today incorporates part of the original structure. In June 1741 the sum of £20 was sent by George Whitfield to John Cennick for the purchase of land and the laying of a foundation stone. Cennick's writings tell us that the stone was laid within ten days of receipt of the money and that prayers and verses were sung upon it. The building was used by colliers and their families as a place of worship.

By the 1840s the building had become inadequate both in size and in décor. Braine's *History of Kingswood Forest* tells us that 'pillars were marbled, the pulpit ornamented with polished pillars for lights, scarlet curtains hung at the south windows and the pews were topped with solid mahogany' but these improvements did little to satisfy the congregation and a decision was made to build a new chapel. Land was acquired in 1850 and the chapel, built to the design of Henry Masters, was opened in 1851. The old meeting house was used as a Sunday school and British Day School until 1905. The building carried a bronze tablet which read 'this building was erected by George Whitfield BA and John Cennick, AD 1741. It is Whitfield's first tabernacle. The oldest existing memorial of his great share in the eighteenth century revival'. Unfortunately the plaque has recently been stolen.

The Tabernacle is a Grade I listed building and the Chapel House Grade II. It is very important that they are retained both for their architectural interest and for their part in the religious revival that changed the world. There is now a preservation trust set up to try and save the buildings and the burial ground for future generations.

The 'new' church was Gothic in style and could seat well in excess of 1,200 people. The acoustic properties of the building were perfect. During the Blitz of 1940 the chapel was damaged and the eastern spire was lost The building is now derelict, following the final service on Sunday 16 October 1983. For a short while the old meeting house was once again used for its original purpose as a place of worship before the congregation combined with members of the Moravian church in Kingswood to form a United Church in 1992.

George Whitfield's schoolroom in Park Road, showing the plaque, high on the wall above the door, that has now been stolen.

The interior of the 'new' Tabernacle, *c.* 1910.

WHITFIELD TABERNACLE
KINGSWOOD.

Right: The 'new' Tabernacle, *c.* 1910.

Below: Chapel House from the burial ground, *c.* 1954. This listed building is now derelict and the graveyard completely overgrown.

Funeral of Fireman Sampson, as reported in *The Western Daily Press*, Monday 22 August 1910:

The funeral took place on Saturday 20 August of fireman R. Samson, for eight years a member of the Kingswood Fire Brigade, who died rather suddenly in a Bristol Hospital from appendicitis.

The procession left the deceased's home headed by Kingswood Mission Silver Band who played the 'Dead March' and proceeded to the Whitfield Tabernacle in which burial ground the internment took place.

The funeral was attended by members of the Kingswood, Keynsham and Mangotsfield Fire Brigades with Captain Williams in charge.

The council were represented by their surveyor (Mr W.D. Bell) and the chief officer. The coffin on which was placed the deceased's helmet was borne on the fire engine.

Many people lined the streets and at the graveside 'Lead Kindly Light' was impressively sung accompanied by the band.

High Street

Above left and right: Advertisement for High Street shops from around 1958.

The crossroads of Regent Street, Park Road, High Street and Hanham Road, *c.* 1968. Blann's hardware store is on the left at the corner of Park Road and Nos 2–14 High Street, known as Kennington Place, with T. W. Jones who sold toys, sweets and tobacco on the corner of Hanham Road.

Above: The junction of Hanham Road with Regent Street and High Street in the 1960s showing T. W. Jones, confectioner and tobacconist, and the Kingswood Hotel.

The stonework of the Kingswood Hotel, now the British Legion, is worth a closer look. On the corner of the building, cut into the stone by a mason just a few years ago are the words PENNY CORNER. During the General Strike the jobless men of Kingswood would gather here and underneath those words is the original inscription, scratched into the stone, which reads PENNYLESS CORNER.

The Monastery of St Joseph, Kingswood. Until 1900, Kingswood's nearest Roman Catholic Church was St Nicholas of Tolentino at Lawford's Gate. In 1900, the creation of a new parish was sanctioned, to be served by the Order of Redemptorist Fathers. A large house with extensive gardens, previously a home for inebriates, was purchased with Mr Pratt, a local Catholic grocer acting as agent. Redemptorist houses are known as monasteries and as such 'The Monastery' appears on local maps of 1904. The house had once belonged to Samuel Budgett. There was an old workhouse standing in the grounds, which he demolished, using the stone to create a boundary wall. The dining room was adapted for use as a chapel which held around sixty people and was open for worship by late January 1901. The first parish priest was Father George Nicholson.

In the summer of 1901, it was decided to purchase an iron-framed building. This was erected next to the house at a cost of approximately £450 including an iron gate and railings. The building could seat 300 people. The seats themselves were bought at 1s 3d each and were the seats from Bristol's redundant horse-drawn trams. The church was opened on the Feast of St Augustine, 29 August 1901, by the Vicar General.

There was a fair amount of anti-Catholic feeling in Kingswood at the time, with lectures being held against the Catholic doctrines in both Whitfield and Wesley schoolrooms. There were also rallies on open space in Bank Road and soon irreverent cartoons appeared in local shop windows but the police were informed and these were removed. Youths regularly gathered outside the church to disrupt the services by banging on the railings. Mr Scully, a burly man, was positioned at the church entrance to keep troublemakers away.

In 1910, the Redemptorists were withdrawn from parish work and the last mass was celebrated at St Josephs, Kingswood on 10 January 1911. In the same month the Bishop of Clifton bought a piece of land in Forest Road, Fishponds and the iron-framed church was taken down and reassembled there.

Budgetts house was vacated and was used as a laundry. During the First World War it became a metal polish factory where the 'Soldiers Friend' was made. It was then used by the Mormons and by the ARP during the Second World War before finally being demolished in 1950 to make way for housing.

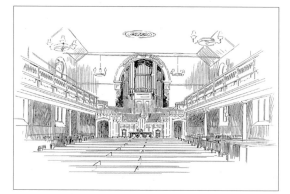

Hanham Road Congregational Church came to be built following a disagreement over the election of a new minister at Whitfield Tabernacle. The church was split and the breakaway group started to meet at a carpenters premises at the bottom of Church Road and then at a blacksmiths in Warmley Hill. The Revd Charles Briggs was invited to Kingswood to conduct a fortnight's services. A marquee was erected and crowds flocked in. It was decided to invite him to stay. A plot of land was secured in Hanham Road and funds and free labour were volunteered. Abraham Fussell was one of the church's founders, giving much time and money to the cause. The foundations of the church were cut on Easter Monday 1868. The chapel was opened by Revd Briggs, followed by a public meeting presided over by Robert Charleton, who bid the church 'God speed'. A fire on 17 May 1898 caused £600 worth of damage and the congregation moved back to Whitfield Tabernacle schoolroom until the building was repaired.

A Whitsuntide procession in the 1960s showing Kingswood Congregational Church banner.

Kingswood and District Nursing Association outgrew the cottage in which it was based. Both living and working conditions had become inadequate. This large house (centre), at the junction of Hanham Road and Woodland Terrace was originally owned by Mrs Elizabeth Douglas. Around the time of the First World War, Mrs Douglas fully equipped her house as a nursing home and handed it over to 'the Nurses of Kingswood' in perpetuity, but eventually the National Health Service decided that it was surplus to requirements and sold it. The proceeds from the sale were put into trust and the profits are now distributed by Kingswood Sickness Relief Trust.

Mrs Rockett, who lived almost next to High Street School, did the sewing for the Nurses Home. She made the uniforms and did the repairs. Matron Frier, the nurse in charge, had seen service in the Boer War. There was also a Welsh district nurse called Nurse Morgan. Local ladies would deal with laying out and confinement and one such lady was Ada Reeves who lived in Wood Road. Her son, Reg, now in his eighties, recalled: 'If a woman went into labour at night, Mother would send me to run through Phipps Alley to the home as she was afraid of the dark!' Phipps Alley ran between Moravian Road and Hanham Road.

Our Lady of Lourdes Roman Catholic Church. Originally, the new Catholic church in Kingswood was supposed to be built on the site of what is now Potterswood Methodist Church. Indeed, the land had already been purchased when it was realised that a larger property, The Woodlands, former home of William Douglas, was for sale. The house, with its extensive grounds, would be perfect for the presbytery and new church. The first mass was celebrated in the house on 20 November 1937. In 1938 building work began on the new church. The contract was awarded to W. Barnes of Liverpool and the workforce boarded with parishioners. They were far from idle – in the evenings they converted many gas-lit homes to electricity.

On 1 October 1938 the church was opened by Bishop Lee. During an air raid on 24 November 1940, land mines were dropped over Kingswood. One landed behind the seven cottages opposite the church, damaging them severely. The church doors were blown in and all of the statues and many of the windows were shattered.

The Catholic Church had never marched in the Kingswood Whitsuntide procession but on 31 May 1976, the congregation from Our Lady of Lourdes joined the Kingswood Whitsuntide procession for the first time.

Opposite above: During 1965, Our Lady of Lourdes Primary School was built and on 5 September 1966, 204 children attended their first day at school. The building was officially opened by the Bishop of Clifton on 4 October 1966. It had been built at a cost of £63,000, the whole cost being met entirely by the Parish.

Opposite below: The Lourdes Social Club successfully ran on the site for many years but eventually both hall and presbytery were replaced. The Woodlands was demolished in 1986.

Arthur H. Skidmore (known as Harry) outside the shop at No. 35 Hanham Road. The shop was opened by Mrs Skidmore in the early 1930s to supplement the family's income. It was Easter time and she started by selling Fry's creme eggs at a halfpenny each. She also made her own ice cream. Mr Derrick, of Court Road, would bring slabs of ice to the shop on his horse and cart. He would use a large hook to lift the ice from the cart. Pieces were then broken down and packed into the outer casing of a double bucket ice cream churn and a paddle would be turned to mix the ice cream.

Mr Skidmore worked as an outworker for Wettons Boot Factory, sewing uppers. He would take them to the factory, at the top of Orchard Road in a little wooden hand cart with metal wheels. He worked from a shed in the back garden, where there was an open fire and a gramophone with a trumpet, where his children would play and listen to 'The Laughing Policeman' as he worked.

The shop at the junction of Court Road and Hanham Road in 1968, still selling sweets and tobacco, owned at that time by J. Hawketts. This was originally one of a pair of cottages (see above) and had a deep well in the back garden.

High Street, Kingswood, *c.* 1903. From the left, Kingswood Grindery Stores, Kingswood Liberal Club and Kingswood Post Office can be seen.

An almost identical view from around 1968 showing Nos 21–27 High Street and the offices of the National Union of Boot and Shoe Operatives.

High Street in around 1907 showing Kingswood Post Office, Bristol Co-operative Society Limited and Greens Circulating Library.

W. J. PETHERICK,
Vice-President Bristol Co-operative Society.

Kingswood Boot Operatives had for many years asked the Co-op to open a branch in the district with one or two tradesmen even offering to sell their premises to the Co-op in order to speed up proceedings. Eventually the Co-op purchased buildings in High Street, Kingswood at a cost of £1,300 and on the afternoon of 22 March 1905, the store was opened, accompanied by a brass band and followed by tea and a public meeting. *The Western Daily Press* the following day gave this report:

> *A tea and concert in connection with the Bristol and District Co-op Society Ltd took place at the Wesleyan Day School, Kingswood, last evening. Mr Carter occupied the chair at the concert and addresses regarding the Co-op movement were given by Miss C.E. May and Mr Petherick. A quartette party, composed of Mrs G. Moon, Mrs E. Bishop, Mr G. Moon and Mr F. Williams rendered glees. A duet was contributed by Mrs Bishop and Mr Moon and vocal solos were supplied by Miss Kate Brecknell and Messrs George Morris, G. Wathen and F. Wilkinson. Mr A.H. Mills was at the piano.*

The first year's profits were £49.00 including sales of £1,035 and expenses of £186. By 1910 profits had risen to £108 from £2,478 sales and £301 expenses.

The Co-op eventually expanded and moved across the street to premises shown in this 1960s photograph.

High Street, Kingswood, c. 1912. The Kings Arms public house is to the left.

The Arch, High Street, c. 1967. This house now forms part of Kingswood Community Centre. In 1866 the Kingswood Horticultural and Flower show was held here. It was also the home of Miss Stone, a teacher at High Street School in the early 1900s.

Left: The Queens Head off-licence with its proprietor Mrs Allen was tied to Bristol United Breweries from 1903. This off-licence was known locally as 'Fat Annies.'

Below: This 1980 photograph shows The Queens Head, now boarded up, J.H. Gapper, butcher and F.P. Newman, wallpaper and paint merchant.

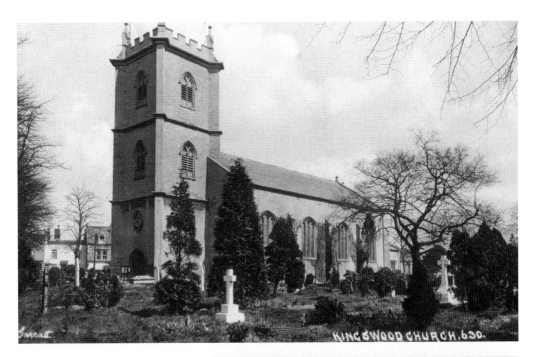

Above and right: Holy Trinity Church Kingswood. The first stone of Holy Trinity Church was laid by the Bishop of Gloucester on 9 June 1819, the stone for the building coming from the quarry at Beech. The church was consecrated on 11 September 1821. It was the first of the 'million fund' churches, a fund of £1 million being set aside by the government in 1818 for church building. More than 2,000 people attended the consecration service. The first marriage at the church was that of Joseph Fletcher of Dursley and Mary Horner of Bitton in November 1822 and the first burial was that of Joseph Smith of Mounthill.

Right: Whitsuntide procession showing the Holy Trinity Church banner, *c.* 1940.

The grounds of Holy Trinity Church, *c.* 1917. Convalescing soldiers, probably from Cossham Hospital, are being entertained. Canon Dandy is on the left in a black hat.

Above left: Poster by Brentnalls of Kingswood for a concert at the Parish Hall in 1914.

Above right: Sunday 11 September 1921, the 100th anniversary of the church, was marked by the unveiling of the War Memorial. It was a wet and windy afternoon but there was a large crowd in attendance. The memorial bears the names of 166 local men killed in the First World War and of sixty-five killed in the Second World War.

Thomas Hooks Shoeing Forge at No. 81 High Street, Kingswood. The squared archway that leads down to what used to be the forge can still be seen today.

The furnace of the forge itself is behind the man in the foreground. Note the huge leather bellows to the left of the picture. The name Hook is written on the anvil in the centre of this picture from around 1910.

Blacksmiths and horses stand in the alleyway leading down to the forge, *c.* 1905. The man holding the horses is William Charles Hook and the man on the far right is Thomas Hook.

Above: High Street, Kingswood, in the early 1900s. The high wall to the left borders the field that is now Kingswood Park.

Below: The field that became Kingswood Park, *c.* 1930. High Street School is in the distance, with the children on their way home playing in the puddles. Kingswood Park was laid out in 1934 to the design of Albert Press, Kingswood's first Parks Superintendent. It has been the scene of many local events including beauty contests, the circus, firework displays and flower shows.

Right: Charles Hawkins started work at
Hanham Colliery as a blacksmith at the age
of thirteen. He then worked for Cooke's
of Bristol where he learnt the ornamental
side of his trade. Soon he decided to try
working for himself and set up business in
the forge at The Barton, Cockroad. He was
just twenty-one when he tendered for the
original set of park gates, with Cllr Cyrus
Whitchurch standing as security for him
as the council thought him far too young
to be able to take on such a job. During
the war, directives came from the Ministry
of Supply to requisition iron railings and
Kingswood Park gates and railings were
under threat. Before they were removed,
Mr Hawkins took a photograph of the
gates and as a result it was possible to
produce an identical set of gates after the
war. By this time Mr Hawkins had moved
to No. 81 High Street, the forge that had
previously been owned by the Hook
family.

Below: The second set of park gates were
opened on 19 April 1947 by Mr H. Miles
and Cllr C. Foxwell.

Left: Charles Hawkins' son, Colin, came into the business in the early 1950s, working with him at High Street, before doing what his father had done and working in the coal mines, this time at Pensford. In the early 1960s, Hawkins forge moved to School Road. Mr Hawkins bought a plot of land and he and Colin built the forge. Colin is now, in 2004, about to retire having taken over the business when his father died. They both did much work that can be seen locally. Charles Hawkins made the gates of Hanham Methodist Church and Colin has just finished a new aviary and the gates and railings for the bowling green at Page Park. He also made the gates and altar rail at Cockroad Chapel.

Below, left: The forge at School Road.

Below, right: Colin Hawkins.

The butchers shop belonging to Arthur Churchill at No. 99 High Street, Kingswood, in the mid-1920s. From left to right: Jeff Savage, Edward Churchill, Sid Davis, Jack Davis, Arthur Churchill and Jennie Churchill.

A.S. Davis & Sons, butchers, at No. 99 High Street (formerly Churchill's). When Arthur died in 1936, Sid Davis, his brother-in-law, took over the shop with his son Dennis. This rank of cottages stood where the Civic Centre now stands.

The demolition of Davis' shop, *c.* 1967.

The High Street in 1967, showing the sweet shop belonging to N. Davis, known as Kerslakes and Priors, where a pet mynah bird lived. The shop was demolished in 1968.

Rosa Wool shop, an agency for Sta-tex dry cleaners at No. 125 High Street. This shop was demolished in 1968 and replaced by the Civic Centre car park.

Opposite below: Kingswood Fire Brigade outside Cossham Hospital, probably around the time of the First World War. The engine is steam operated. One of the firemen would have been the stoker, keeping the fire going. This in turn produced enough pressure to pump 300-400 gallons of water per minute. During the days of horse-drawn engines, Melvyn Hobbs, who lived in Alma Road, was caller for the fire station. The horses were kept in a field in what is now Kingswood Park so, firstly, he had to summon the men, then they had to catch and harness the horses, before they went to the fire. Their job was made more difficult by Melvyn who would reputedly often go and tell his family and friends about the fire before he fetched the fire brigade!

This is the earliest known photograph of Kingswood Fire Brigade, taken outside Kingswood fire station which stood between Hollow Road and High Street School. The appliance is a horse-drawn manual fire engine with a pump operated by poles which can just be seen under the feet of the firemen. These were hinged and opened out fore and aft of the engine. Teams of men would pump these poles in a rocker movement, rather like a see saw. This in turn would pump water through valves in the engine and out through the side of the appliance. The pressure would only have been enough to produce about 100 gallons of water per minute and it was a very exhausting task.

Kingswood Fire Brigade, c. 1927. Harry Bamford was the driver of this Merryweather 250-gallon 'Hatfield' motor fire engine. The Kingswood brigade had gone through hard times prior to the delivery of this engine. The district council had received complaints from the brigade about shortages of equipment and for a while it was disbanded.

Kingswood Fire Brigade with the Merryweather 'Hatfield' motor fire engine, c. 1930.

Kingswood district council offices. This building stood next to High Street School and this photograph clearly shows the arches, now partially bricked up, of the old Kingswood fire station.

The council offices in 1986, boarded up and ready for demolition.

Above: The Park School, or High Street School as it was originally known, was opened on 21 May 1892 by the Rt Hon. H. Campbell-Bannerman. It was built from pennant stone with Bath stone dressings at a cost of approximately £6,000, with furnishings costing a further £1,350. The building work was carried out by Mr J. Perrott of Wellington Road, St Pauls. During the First World War, many ex-High Street Boys were called up. Sixty-eight of those boys and one member of staff did not return. Their names were honoured on a school war memorial. In 2002 the school was closed and now a new school building has been built behind the original one.

Left: Rebie Fudge aged five, as High Street School May Queen, *c.* 1920.

A class group at
High Street School,
sometime before 1910.

Kingswood Junior
Boys football team,
c. 1949.

Park School second
team 1969. From left
to right, back row:
Mr Jeffries, John Press,
Paul Bridgeman, Keith
Dodd, Neil Smart,
Martin Fey. Middle
Row: Mickey Harris,
Steve Burnham,
Richard Lovell, Pete
Yeoman, Glyn Owen.
Front row: Steve Wade,
Kelvin Parry.

KINGSWOOD TERMINUS.

This page and opposite: Kingswood Tramway Terminus from a drawing by F.G. Lewin, prolific postcard artist (left, top). The electric line to Kingswood was opened on Monday 14 October 1895 and at 12.30 p.m., car No. 89, carrying William Butler, George White and other distinguished guests lead a procession of eight decorated tram cars from Old Market to Kingswood. The journey took approximately thirty minutes. Speeches were made at the terminus and the dignitaries were returned to St George's depot for a tour of the power station and then back to Old Market, from where they were taken by carriage to the Grand Hotel where lunch was served. The Tramway Company had also arranged other festivities which included a meat dinner for 1,200 aged and deserving inhabitants of Kingswood and St George. All who attended the meal were given special tickets for free tram rides. The day was given the status of a virtual public holiday with local factories and schools closing at midday. In the evening many of the major buildings along the route were illuminated and fireworks lit the night sky. The Tramway Depot (opposite, top) itself was situated on High Street almost opposite where Kingswood Library now stands.

Left: A tram outside the depot, 4 August 1938.

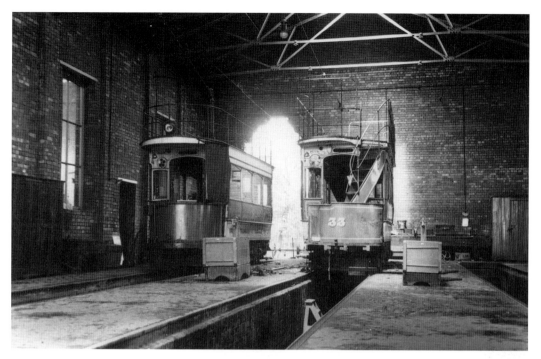

Interior of the tramshed, 4 August 1939. A hole had been cut in the back of the shed and temporary tracks laid to allow the trams to be taken out into the field beyond to be scrapped.

At the terminus, looking down Hill street showing tram car No. 86, 21 August 1939.

In 1938, many of Bristol's trams were retired. Kingswood depot was converted to become a breaking yard with scrap sidings laid on the allotments at the rear. A huge hole was made in the shed wall and tracks extended onto the sidings. The 'funeral run' was not popular with local people. Trams on their way to be broken were often mobbed and many received such extensive damage that they had to be towed to the depot. There was space on the sidings for forty trams and they were destroyed at the rate of one per day. Top-deck seats were sold as garden benches and the trams themselves were burnt. Any metal that was left was sold as scrap. During the air raid of 11 April 1941, the St Phillip's Bridge power station was bombed and all power to the trams was cut. The last tram to Kingswood was heading home to the depot. Just past the clock tower the lights went out. Without electricity there was nothing for it but to push. The driver and conductor, Mr Webster and Mr Brittan, along with one or two passers-by, soon had the tram moving. The handbrake wasn't applied until the tram had swung through the gates and into the depot. The raid brought an end to Bristol Tramway. All remaining cars were towed to Kingswood depot and destroyed.

Above, left: Breaking up trams at Kingswood, *c.* 1939. By 1942 some 264 tons of tracking lying in the main Kingswood and Hanham roads were taken up and salvaged by the Bristol Tramways & Carriage Co.

Above, right: During the First World War young ladies became 'clippies' on the trams, in place of the men who had been called up. This is Miss Evelyn Rockett of Kingswood in her uniform.

The tramway shed during its demolition in 1988.

A large assembly shed was erected on the site of the tramway sidings in 1941 to undertake the production of army vehicles. At peak production, 240 vehicles per week were built. This included jeeps, snow ploughs and up to 40-ton tank transporters. Some 44,000 vehicles were produced in all. Lex Tillotson eventually moved onto the site which has since been built on and is now known as Crates Court.

Looking down Hill Street, Kingswood, with the tramway terminus to the left, 1920s.

Right: Henry Attwell's bakery was established in 1890 and delivered bread and cakes throughout the Kingswood area. The bakery was situated at No. 27 Hill Street, Kingswood. Honey Way now stands on the site.

Below: Henry Attwell's delivery cart, with Clifford Smart holding the horse, *c.* 1910.

Other local titles published by Tempus

Stapleton
VERONICA SMITH

Illustrated with over 200 photographs, this pictorial history is a remarkable evocation of life in and around the Stapleton of yesteryear. From timeless vistas of the Frome Valley to snapshots of the bandstand at Eastville Park, local sporting heroes at Alexandra Park, Fishponds Lido and Coronation Day parties, this volume provides a nostalgic insight into the life and changing landscape of the area around Stapleton.
7524 3059 9

Filton Voices
JANE TOZAR AND JACKIE SIMS

This book brings together the personal memories of people who lived and worked in Filton from the 1930s, vividly recalling the farms and fields before they were lost to housing. The voices tell of childhood games, the close-knit community, shops and entertainment, as well as the devastating effects of bombing raids on the aircraft factory, cheek by jowl with the village. The stories are complemented by a hundred photographs drawn from the private collections of the contributors.
7524 3097 1

Haunted Bristol
SUE LE'QUEUX

This selection of newspaper reports and first-hand accounts recalls strange and spooky happenings in Bristol's ancient streets, churches, theatres and public houses. From paranormal manifestations at The Bristol Old Vic to the ghostly activity of a grey monk who is said to haunt Bristol's twelfth-century Cathedral, this spine-tingling collection of supernatural tales is sure to appeal to anyone interested in Bristol's haunted heritage.
7524 3300 8

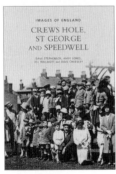

Crews Hole, St George and Speedwell
DAVE STEPHENSON, DAVE CHEESLEY, JILL WILLMOTT AND ANDY JONES

Illustrated with over 200 archive pictures, this collection evocatively captures the histories of Netham, Crews Hole, St George and Speedwell in east Bristol. Snapshots of everyday life combine with vistas of the industries upon which these communities relied, particularly the collieries and chemical works whose chimneys towered over this area of the city. This fascinating volume shows the great changes which have taken place in commerce, heavy industry, transport and residential areas.
0 7524 2948 5

If you are interested in purchasing other books published by Tempus, or in case you have difficulty finding any Tempus books in your local bookshop, you can also place orders directly through our website

www.tempus-publishing.com